New CLAIT
Unit 2
Word Processing
The Course Book

CGP's Course Books offer a step-by-step approach
to help you really get to grips with New CLAIT.

Each topic is explained using everyday language,
with plenty of worked examples, handy hints and practical tasks.

Exactly what you need —
perfect for even the most 'computer-phobic' learners.

CONTENTS

Published by Coordination Group Publications

Contributors:
Jo Anson
Charley Darbishire
Dominic Hall
Simon Little
John Robinson
Rachel Selway
Jennifer Underwood

ISBN 1 84146 325 6

Endorsed by OCR for use with OCR Level 1 Certificate for IT users-
New CLAIT specification.
Groovy website: www.cgpbooks.co.uk
With thanks to Rebecca May and Ray Davies for the proof-reading.
Jolly bits of clipart from CorelDRAW.
Printed by Elanders Hindson, Newcastle upon Tyne.
With thanks to Microsoft for permission to use screenshots from
MS Word XP and MS Windows XP.

Text, design, layout and original illustrations © Coordination Group Publications 2004.

What is New CLAIT?

Here's a page to let you know what this book is all about.

New CLAIT is a Computer Course for Beginners

In New CLAIT, you'll learn how to make computers work for you, so you can use things like:

- word processors — to write letters
- spreadsheets — to do your household accounts
- databases — to organise information
- e-mail — to keep in touch with people all over the world
- the Internet — to find information

Just Have a Go, You Won't Break it

The key to learning about computers is to try things.
Don't be afraid of it — you won't break the computer with a mouse and keyboard.
You'd need to open it up and pour a cup of tea inside to break it.

This book will take you through everything
step-by-step. You'll be doing things all the time.

When you've got to do things,
you'll find numbered shapes like this.

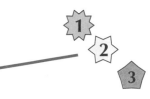

There are also practice exercises at the end of each section,
so you can see how you'd do in a real New CLAIT test.

Read this bit if you are a Tutor

1) We've used Office XP and Windows XP Professional for this
   book, but most things will be the same for older versions.

2) To keep things simple we've concentrated on one way of doing things instead
   of confusing people with five different ways to do the same thing.

3) There is a CD which accompanies this series of books. It contains all the files the student
   will need for the worked examples, practice exercises and exams. It also contains sample
   answer files for most of the exercises. The files have been saved in Word 95 format for
   maximum compatibility. In the OCR assessment they'll be in .txt format.

Relax — computers are fun...

This book tells you everything you need to pass New CLAIT Unit 2. Section 1 also gives
you a quick reminder of the basic computer skills you'll need for the New CLAIT course.

The Bits of a Computer

You're probably familiar with this stuff by now, but just in case you've forgotten, here's a quick reminder of what each bit of the computer actually does.

The Parts of a Computer Do Different Jobs

Here's a computer — and all its bits are labelled.

Monitor — looks like a TV screen. What you're working on is displayed on it.

System box — the 'brain' of the computer, where all the bits and pieces that make it work can be found. You put CDs and disks in here, and plug all the other computer parts into the back.

Printer — used to make a paper copy of what's on your screen, like letters or photos.

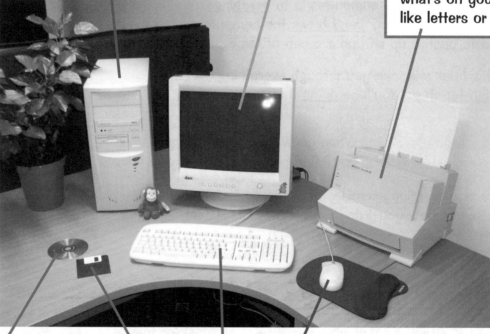

Compact discs (CDs) and floppy disks — can be used to store your work. You can put them into a different computer and your work will appear.

Mouse — when you move this over your desk, a little arrow on the screen will move too. You can use it to select and change different things on the screen.

Keyboard — has keys with letters and numbers on that you press to enter information, e.g. to write a letter.

I wonder what the toy monkey does...

Soft toys are an optional part of computer equipment, and they have no function whatsoever. You might find it useful to learn what all the other bits do, though.

The Bits of a Computer

The most important bits of a computer are hidden inside it.

Computers come in Different Shapes and Sizes

Laptops are handy little computers that you can fold up, carry about in a bag and use anywhere, like on the train, if you like. They're as good as normal computers, just smaller.

Notebooks are like laptops, but smaller and a bit less powerful. (Still plenty good enough for us normal folks though.)

Computers are made of Hardware and Software

HARDWARE is all the physical bits of a computer that you can see and touch — not just obvious bits like the monitor, keyboard and printer, but also all the bits and bobs inside that make it work.

SOFTWARE is all the programs in a computer that make it do different things — i.e. the instructions that tell the computer what to do. You can buy new software on CDs.

For example, 'Microsoft Word' is a program which lets you write letters and things. A computer game is another program, where the keys you press might guide a character round a special world. Nice.

Here are Some Terms You'll Need to Know

1) Programs, like 'Microsoft Word' or 'Microsoft Excel', are usually called applications.

2) Files are made by using applications. They contain the things you make — e.g. a file from a word-processor, like 'Microsoft Word', will be lots of text, and a file from a drawing program will be a picture.

3) A folder is a place where you can store files or applications. They're really useful for organising your computer.

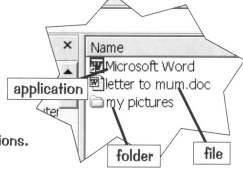

'Microsoft Windows' is a special program called an 'operating system' — it lets you interact with the computer, e.g. open and close other applications, and generally control what's going on — useful.

Programs like 'Microsoft Windows' let you do loads of things without having to understand what's really going on.

I thought hardware was nuts and bolts...

Don't worry too much if you don't know a lot about what's inside a computer. The most important part is knowing how to use a computer properly, and making it work for you.

Using the Keyboard

Ah, the keyboard. You'll be seeing a lot more of the keyboard in this book.

All Keyboards Look the Same (More or Less)

The big bit with the letters on is always the same — it's the same arrangement as on a typewriter. So if you've used a typewriter before, you should pick it up really easily.

Don't worry about these keys. They're called <u>function keys</u> and do special things in different programs.

These are <u>navigation keys</u>, and do things like taking you to the start or end of your work. Don't worry about most of these — you won't use many apart from '<u>Delete</u>'.

These little arrow keys are called <u>cursor keys</u>. They let you move through a piece of work so that you can work on different bits.

You'll need these <u>text keys</u> the most. They're for letters and numbers, so they're really useful for typing. (This is the bit that's like a typewriter.)

This is the <u>numeric key pad</u>. It's a bit like a calculator, with numbers and maths symbols.

Get those fingers moving...

As you start remembering where different letters and symbols are on the keyboard, you'll find it a lot easier to type things. You'll probably make fewer mistakes too.

Using the Keyboard

Here are some of the keys that'll come in really handy later on in the book.

Some Keys are Really Special

Here are some of the keys you'll find really useful when you're typing:

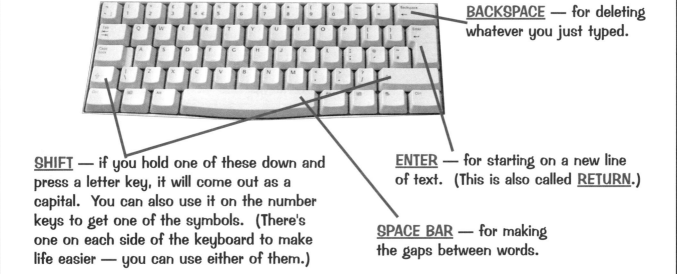

BACKSPACE — for deleting whatever you just typed.

SHIFT — if you hold one of these down and press a letter key, it will come out as a capital. You can also use it on the number keys to get one of the symbols. (There's one on each side of the keyboard to make life easier — you can use either of them.)

ENTER — for starting on a new line of text. (This is also called **RETURN**.)

SPACE BAR — for making the gaps between words.

Have a Go at Using the Keyboard

Learning to type is really slow to begin with, but you'll soon get better with practice. If you need a bit more practice, have a look at New Clait Unit 1 — Using a Computer.

 Open a word-processing application and have a go at typing:

- Make sure you're typing accurately. It doesn't matter if you're slow.
- You don't have to whack the keys — find out how lightly you can press a key to still make it work.
- Make sure you know how to use the four special keys above.

Have a cocktail at the space bar...

You'll be spending a lot of time using the keyboard in this book, so get used to using all those special keys now. You can't just ignore them and hope they'll go away.

Get Used to the Mouse

Nope, it's not furry — sorry to disappoint you.
You're probably quite used to using it by now, but here's a quick reminder in case you've forgotten.

First, Catch Your Mouse...

This is a mouse.

This is its right button
(which you won't need for now).

This is its left button.

This is a mouse mat.

The mouse has a nice <u>rounded top</u> that you put your palm on,
and a couple of <u>buttons</u> at the top where your fingers go. Like this:

...Then Push it Around a bit

1) To use your mouse, all you have to do is <u>push</u> it around on your desk.
    (You'll find that it <u>glides</u> along nicely on top of a foamy <u>mouse mat</u>.)

2) Underneath the mouse will be a little <u>ball</u> or a little <u>red light</u>.
    This bit tells the computer how you are <u>moving</u> the mouse.

3) As you move the mouse, a little <u>arrow</u> on your screen moves about.
    This arrow is called a <u>pointer</u> or a <u>cursor</u>.

Pointers look a bit like this.
(But they're about ten times <u>tinier</u>.)

When you're using <u>writing software</u>, like 'Microsoft
Word', your cursor will look like this, but a lot smaller.

Don't worry if your pointer looks <u>different</u> to the ones above. It'll be really obvious —
the pointer is the thing that <u>moves about</u> on your screen when you move the mouse.

Don't let your mouse get covered in fluff...

That's cruelty to animals, that is. To keep your mouse working well, use it on
a nice flat surface, and don't let the underneath get too dirty and disgusting.

Get Used to the Mouse

Using the mouse is a vital computer skill. Make sure you've got it right.

You'll need to use the Left Mouse Button all the time

You normally just 'click' the mouse button — give it a quick press
and then take your finger off again — you'll hear a little clicking noise.

- The left mouse button 'selects' things. This means that when you move the pointer over
  something and click your left mouse button, you'll make it 'alive' and useable.

- If you 'double-click' the left mouse button — quickly click on something twice —
  you'll be able to open whatever it is (e.g. a file or application) and use it.

Try this Quick Activity for Learning Mouse Control

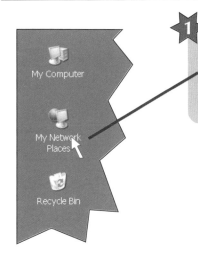

 Move the mouse around until the
pointer on the screen is on top of
an icon. (An icon is a little picture,
representing a file or application.)

Click the left mouse button once.
The icon will get darker — become
highlighted. This means you have
selected it.

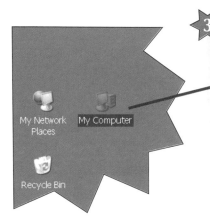

Move the pointer over a different
icon. Press the left mouse button
down and keep it held down. Then
move your mouse and you'll find you
can drag the icon about. Useful.

 If you 'double-click' on an icon (move your pointer to
it and do a quick 'click click'), you'll make it open.

Clickety click, click click... hours of fun...

It takes a bit of practice to double-click — the two clicks have to be quite close together.
What you've got to remember is — left once selects, left twice opens, left-hold-move drags.

Word-Processing Basics

Word-processing is all about text, and the things you can do with it.
Get ready for lots of typing.

A Text Editor is very Basic

You can type in a <u>text editor</u>, like '<u>Windows Notepad</u>'
but you can only make <u>basic changes</u> to the way the text looks.
You <u>won't</u> use it much, but it's a good way to start learning about <u>entering text</u>.

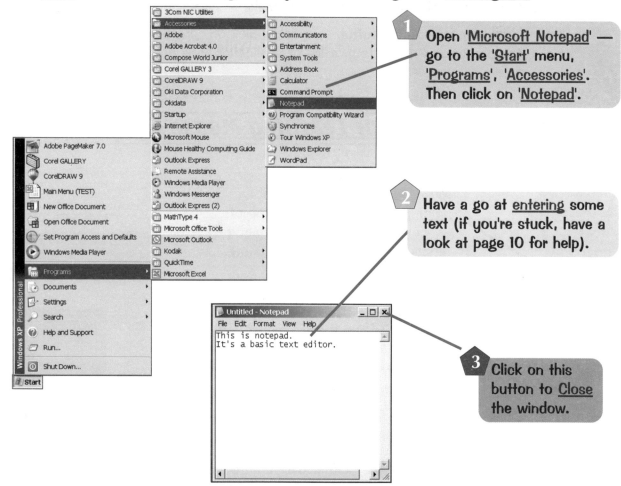

1 Open '<u>Microsoft Notepad</u>' —
go to the '<u>Start</u>' menu,
'<u>Programs</u>', '<u>Accessories</u>'.
Then click on '<u>Notepad</u>'.

2 Have a go at <u>entering</u> some
text (if you're stuck, have a
look at page 10 for help).

3 Click on this
button to <u>Close</u>
the window.

Word-Processors make your Text look Good

Word-processors are different from text editors, because
they let you change the way your text looks on the page.

1)   Word-processors let you choose <u>different ways</u> to <u>present</u> your text, like
      making it **bold**, or putting it in the centre of the page. This is called <u>formatting</u>.

2)   They can even do <u>fancy things</u> like adding <u>pictures</u>, or <u>checking</u> spelling and grammar.

3)   One of the most <u>common</u> word-processors is '<u>Microsoft Word</u>'.
      You may see others, e.g. <u>WordPerfect</u>. They all work in a similar way.

Word-processors are more fun than text editors...

You can't do much more than type text in a text editor, so it's hard to produce nice documents.
A word-processor can do a lot more things to make your text look good.

Word-Processing Basics

You'll learn how to change the look of your text later on in the book, but here are some examples of things you can do to make your document look interesting.

Word-Processors make your Text look Good

There are lots of things you can <u>do</u> to <u>text</u> in a word-processor application like Microsoft Word:

Make words <u>different</u> sizes

Write in <u>different</u> <u>colours</u>

Make words **bold**

<u>Underline</u> words

Make words *italic*

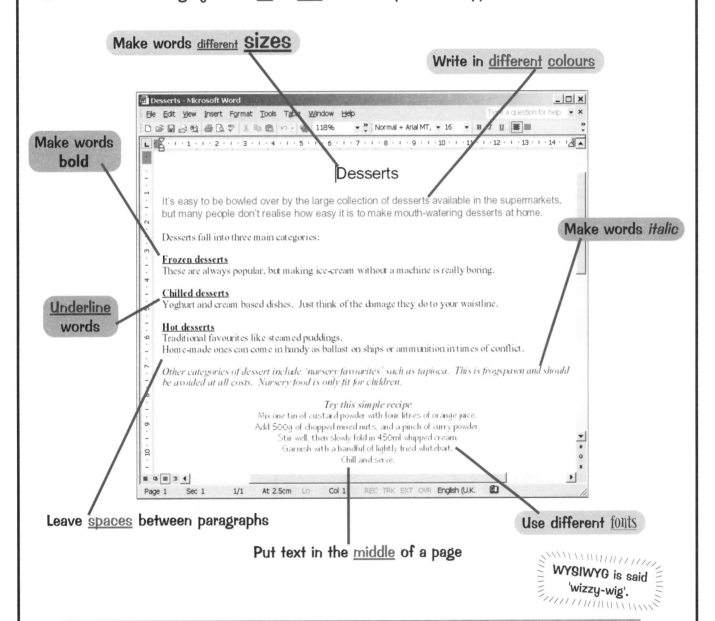

Leave <u>spaces</u> between paragraphs

Put text in the <u>middle</u> of a page

Use different <u>fonts</u>

WYSIWYG is said 'wizzy-wig'.

A word-processor is usually '<u>WYSIWYG</u>' (<u>What You See Is What You Get</u>) software. This means that when you print your document it'll look just like it did on the screen.

That looks great, but how do I do all this stuff?

Good question. Well, that's what the rest of this book is all about.
It shows you how to do this kind of thing — so keep reading to find out more.

Entering Text Correctly

You may have already learnt how to enter text. Here's a quick reminder anyway.

Just Press a Key to Enter a Letter

 1 Open a new 'Microsoft Word' document (look at the Unit 1 book if you've forgotten how).

2 Type 'my favourite dessert is mousse' (use the space bar to make spaces between the words).

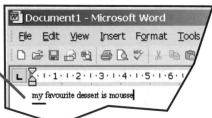

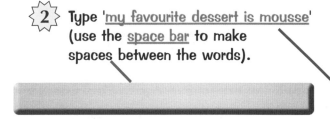

3 Now press 'Enter' (the 'Return' key) to go to a new line.

Use 'Shift' for Capital Letters and Symbols

Hold down the 'Shift' key when you're typing to get capital letters, or to get the top character when there's two characters on one key.

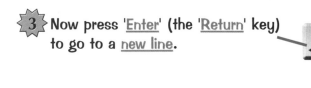

4 Type your name (hold down the 'Shift' key to get a capital letter).

5 Put an exclamation mark at the end — hold down 'Shift' and press '1'.

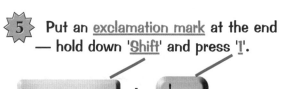

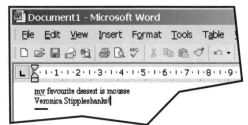

It should all come flooding back...

If you're confident about entering text, then this page was probably nice and relaxing.
If you need to refresh your memory, don't panic — just look at our Unit 1 book, Section 3.

Entering Text Correctly

You can Delete Text

If you want to <u>delete</u> anything, use the '<u>Backspace</u>' or '<u>Delete</u>' keys.

> '<u>Backspace</u>' deletes the character to the <u>left</u> of the cursor.
> '<u>Delete</u>' deletes the character to the <u>right</u> of the cursor.

 1 Carrying on with the Word document from page 10, use the <u>mouse</u> or <u>cursor</u> <u>keys</u> to put the <u>cursor</u> at the end of the last line (it might be there <u>already</u>).

2 Press '<u>Backspace</u>' to delete the exclamation mark.

 3 Use the <u>mouse</u> or <u>cursor keys</u> to put the cursor in front of your name, and press the '<u>Delete</u>' key until your name has <u>disappeared</u>.

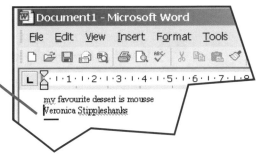

 4 <u>Close</u> Microsoft Word. Click on '<u>No</u>' when it asks if you want to <u>save</u> the changes you made.

You Need to be Really Accurate

You have to enter a <u>lot</u> of <u>text</u> in the assessment, and if you're not <u>accurate</u> you'll <u>lose marks</u>.

1) <u>Watch out</u> for mistakes like an <u>extra space</u> between words or lines, <u>spelling mistakes</u>, or even <u>words</u> or <u>sentences</u> <u>missed out</u>.

2) Also watch out for <u>full stops</u> and <u>commas</u>. You need to put <u>one</u> or <u>two</u> spaces after them. It doesn't <u>matter</u> if you use one or two, but try to make it the same in each document.

> <u>Remember</u>
> 1) Print your document.
> 2) Check it against the original text.
> 3) Highlight the mistakes.
> 4) Change it on your computer.
> 5) Print it again.
> 6) Check it again.

It's easy to make typing errers, oops, errors...

Everyone makes mistakes when they type, but be as accurate as you can.
Type carefully, and read through your work afterwards to look for mistakes.

Using Files

This is another bit that you might remember from Unit 1.
There's no escaping from the 'File' menu this time round, anyway.

Use the File Menu to Open, Close, Save and Print

It's easy to use the file menu — when you're in 'Microsoft Word', you just click on the 'File' menu, move your mouse down to the command you need, and click on it.

These are the only commands you'll need in Unit 2.

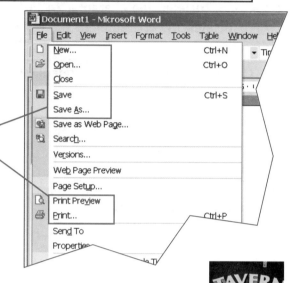

Create Documents

 Open 'Microsoft Word'.

 It will automatically create a new blank document for you.

 Type your name and address.

This isn't a file menu.
Don't click on it.

Print your Work

 Click on 'Print Preview' from the 'File' menu to see exactly what your document will look like when you print it.
Just click on 'Close' when you've finished looking.

 Then click on 'Print' from the 'File' menu to print the document.

 You should see this screen — if you're happy with the printing options, click 'OK'.

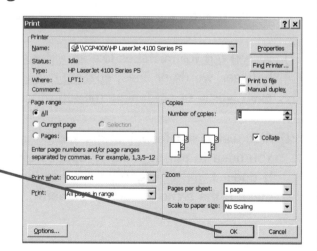

It's a whistle-stop tour of the 'File' menu...

There's a lot to cover on these pages. If it's all a bit of a blur, don't panic — get hold of a copy of the first book, Unit 1, and re-read Sections 2 and 4 until you're confident.

Using Files

Save your Work

1 <u>Save</u> your document by clicking on '<u>Save</u>' in the 'File' menu.
You'll get a new window like this:

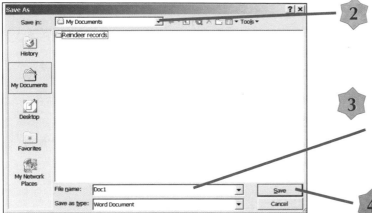

2 Click on the <u>arrow</u> to choose <u>where</u> to save your file.

3 <u>Delete</u> the text that's in this box (it'll probably be 'Doc 1').
Then type in your document's <u>name</u> — call it '<u>Address</u>'.

4 Click on '<u>Save</u>'.

Save another Version of your Work

 Save a <u>second version</u> of your file
— click on '<u>Save As</u>' in the 'File' menu.
Now repeat steps 2 to 4 from above, but
name your document '<u>Address Version 2</u>'.

It's best to store your work
on the computer, not on
your desk.

'Save As' comes in handy when you've
made changes to a document but you
want to keep the old version as well.

Close and Open Files

 <u>Close</u> 'Address Version 2' by clicking '<u>Close</u>' in the 'File' menu.

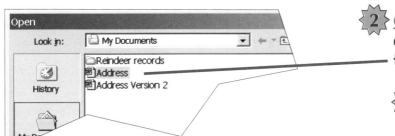

2 <u>Open</u> your old file, 'Address' —
click '<u>Open</u>' in the 'File' menu,
then <u>double-click</u> on the file.

3 Click on '<u>Close</u>' in the 'File'
menu to <u>close</u> 'Address'.

And relax...

You're probably fed up with all that clicking — but it's worth learning the basic stuff properly,
so you don't have problems when it gets trickier later on.

Section Two — Practice Exercises

Here's some nice word-processing practice for you. I'm afraid there's loads of typing to do.

Exercise 1

1.   Create a new word processing document.

2.   Enter the following text.

> THE INTERNET
>
> If you connect a number of computers together you can create what is known as a "network". The Internet is a huge network of connected computers across the whole world. It was created in the 1960s. These computers can be connected together using normal telephone lines, fibre optic cables, satellite and microwave links. When you are connected to the Internet you can then communicate or talk with other computers and exchange information.
>
> Instead of writing a letter, a report or just a note and putting it into an envelope, then buying a stamp and finally posting the letter, you can use the Internet to send and receive emails. You can also use the Internet to browse or search for information. The World Wide Web (www) is a collection of information in multimedia form on the Internet. This information is stored at locations called websites, in the form of web pages.

3.   Check through your work and correct any obvious errors.

4.   Enter your name, centre number and today's date a few lines below the end of the text.

5.   Save the document with the filename **internet**.

6.   Preview your work before printing out one copy.

7.   Close the document and exit the application securely.

Exercise 2

1.   Open the word processing document called **internet**.

2.   Delete **It was created in the 1960s.** from the first paragraph.
     Remember to delete the full stop and the extra spaces.

3.   Delete **or talk** from the last sentence in the first paragraph.

4.   Change (**www**) to be in capital letters, (**WWW**), in the second paragraph.

5.   Save the document with the new filename **internet 2**.

6.   Preview your work then print one copy.

7.   Close the document and exit the application securely.

Section Two — Practice Exercises

Yep, there are even more things to type and delete on this page.
Don't forget to check your work for mistakes.

Exercise 3

1. Create a new word processing document.

2. Enter the following text.

> THE LAKE DISTRICT
>
> The Lake District National Park was created in 1961. It covers 885 square miles. It is the largest of the 11 national parks in England and Wales. It contains many miles of paths and bridleways through beautiful countryside. There are impressive mountains, rolling fells, relaxing lakes and busy market towns.
>
> The area around Grasmere, Ambleside, Coniston and Windermere forms the main centre for tourist activity during the busy summer months. This is the ideal base for cycling, walking and boating holidays. The area is also steeped in literary history. A good starting point is the National Park Visitors Centre at Brockhole. There are well kept gardens, an adventure playground for the kids and useful information on walks, talks and events throughout the area.

3. Check through your work and correct any obvious errors.

4. Enter your name, centre number and today's date a few lines below the end of the text.

5. Save the document with the filename **lakes**.

6. Preview your work before printing out one copy.

7. Close the document and exit the application securely.

Exercise 4

1. Open the word processing document **lakes.**

2. Change the year in the first sentence from **1961** to **1951**.

3. Delete **and bridleways** from the first paragraph.

4. In the second paragraph, delete the sentence which begins **The area is also steeped...**

5. Insert the following text after the words **beautiful countryside** in the first paragraph

    ...which can be enjoyed on foot, on a horse or on a bicycle.

6. Save the document with the new filename **lakes 2**.

7. Preview your work then print one copy.

8. Close the document and exit the application securely.

Selecting Text

If you want to make changes to a word, a sentence or a paragraph in your document, first you need to select the text you want to change. There are different ways of doing this.

You Can Select Text by Clicking and Dragging

Here's how to click and drag to select text:

 Open the document 'Slug Collectors Monthly'.

 Press the left mouse button in front of the word 'relevant'.

 Keep the left mouse button held down, and move it to the right until the word 'relevant' is highlighted in black, like this:

> **Slug Collectors Monthly**
> The next meeting of the Slug Collectors' Society will be held on the 14th June.
> All members with a new species to report should fill in the relevant paperwork beforehand.
> If you are bringing slugs with you, please ensure that you wipe the slime off the chairs afterwards.

You can Select Text with the 'Shift' Key

 Click the left mouse button at the beginning of the first line.

> **Slug Collectors Monthly**
> The next meeting of the Slug Collectors' Society will be held on the 14th June.
> All members with a new species to report should fill in the relevant paperwork beforehand.
> If you are bringing slugs with you, please ensure that you wipe the slime off the chairs afterwards.

 Press down the 'Shift' key (don't let go).

 Now click the mouse at the end of the paragraph. This will select everything between the first and the second click.

 Let go of the 'Shift' key. Now click once anywhere in the window to deselect the text.

 Try selecting other bits of text — click at the beginning, hold down 'Shift', then click at the end.

Selecting text can be a real drag...

You might find it easier to select text using the cursor keys rather than clicking and dragging or using shift — you'll find out how on the next page.

Selecting Text

Sometimes it's hard to select things accurately using the mouse —
the cursor keys let you highlight exactly what you want.

You can Select Text using the Cursor Keys

 Put the cursor at the beginning
of the second sentence in the
second paragraph.

 Hold down the 'shift' key,
and keep it held down.

Slug Collectors Monthly
The next meeting of the Slug Collectors' Society will be held on the 14th June.
All members with a new species to report should fill in the relevant paperwork beforehand.
If you are bringing slugs with you, please ensure that you wipe the slime off the chairs afterwards.

Annual Outing
This year's outing was to a field near Slough. The coach set off early, and there was a lot of excitement in the air as we approached our destination. The dew was still on the grass when we arrived, which led to a record number of sightings. We were delighted to see that Sybil the big black slug was still in residence, and we made the acquaintance of many of her charming offspring. We look forward to seeing many more of them next year.

 Press the right cursor key to select one character at a time.

'Character' just means a single letter, number or symbol.

 Now hold down the right
cursor key to move faster,
until you've selected the
whole sentence.

If you highlight too much, just use the 'left' cursor key to go back.

You can Select Text Line by Line

 Click at the beginning of the first line in the first paragraph.

 Hold down the 'Shift' key, and press the 'down arrow' cursor key.

 Press it three times to highlight the first three lines.

Every time you click the 'down' cursor key, another line of text is highlighted.

Slug Collectors Monthly
The next meeting of the Slug Collectors' Society will be held on the 14th June.
All members with a new species to report should fill in the relevant paperwork beforehand.
If you are bringing slugs with you, please ensure that you wipe the slime off the chairs afterwards.

 Close the file. Click on 'No' when it asks if you want to save the changes you made.

Now you've selected your text, you can change it...

You need to get confident about selecting text. Once you've selected it, you can do loads of things, like make it bold or italic, or move it around the page. The next pages show you how...

Fonts

A font is like a style of handwriting. Using different fonts can make things look professional, friendly, stylish, funny, evil, stupid, erm... and more.

Here are Some Fonts You Might Find Useful

Life would be pretty boring if all writing looked the same, so there are thousands of different styles of text to choose from. These are called fonts.
Here's a selection of the best (well, my favourites* anyway):

This font is called Times New Roman.	A professional, newspaper-style font. For formal letters and stuffy things.
This font is called Arial.	A friendlier font than Times New Roman, but still quite formal. You'll find this font in books and magazines.
This font is called Taffy.	This font looks a bit like neat handwriting. It would look good on informal posters, or as a note on the bottom of something.
This font is called Litterbox.	A font that's very much like handwriting. Mostly useful for posters and arty things.
This font is called Alleycat.	A very stylish font. You can imagine this on shop signs or posh magazines.
This font is called Courier.	This font looks like it came from a typewriter. It's pretty ugly really.

Fonts can b f   ju   have a go
When you start typing in Word, it'll probably come out in Times New Roman — such a boring font. Well, read on to find out how to change to the more exciting ones.

Section Three — Changing the Appearance of a Document

Fonts

When you've read this page, you'll be able to make stunning pieces of writing with different fonts.

Changing Fonts is Easy Peasy

Now you're going to learn how to change fonts when you're writing in Word.

 Open Word and do a little bit of typing.

 You'll see a box at the top which tells you which font you're currently using. Click on the arrow next to it.

You'll get a menu of all the different fonts you can use.

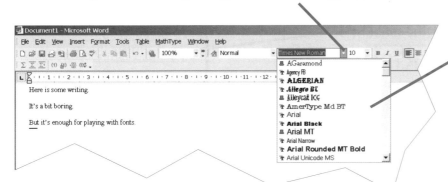

In later versions of Word, the font names are written in their own font. So you'll know exactly what your writing will look like.

3 Click on the font you'd like to use. Simple.

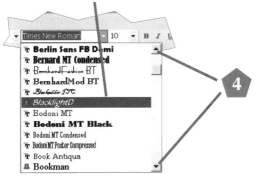

Click and hold on these arrows to look through the rest of the fonts in the menu.

5 Then do some more typing. Ta da — the words will come out in your new font.

It's a bit boring.

But it's enough for playing with fonts.

Ooh look, this is a new font... Brilliant.

You can Change Fonts After you've Typed things

 Select the piece of text you want to change. (See pages 16 and 17 for how to select text.)

 Then change the font in the same way as you did in steps 2 to 4.

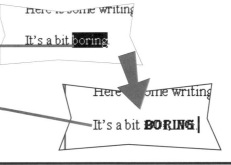

Here is some writing

It's a bit **boring**.

Here is some writing

It's a bit **BORING**.

Isn't this amazing... just fantastic...

Once you get the hang of it, you'll have a great time playing with fonts.
You'll be stealing people's things just so you can write them multi-fonted ransom notes...

Bold, Italics and Underline

You've learnt how to make some changes to your text, but there's still loads more things you can do to make your text more exciting. Like bold, italics and underline. Wa-hoo.

Sometimes You Need to Make Text Stand Out

Bold, italics and underlining are useful ways of emphasising important words or phrases.

Bold is where your writing looks thicker and heavier.

Italics are when the text is slanted a bit to the right.

Underlining is used for titles, and for making things stand out in general. (Look at the amount of underlining in this book, for example...)

If you're feeling adventurous, you could make combinations of bold, underlining and italics. Wow.

> This text is normal.
>
> **This text is bold.**
>
> *This text is in italics.*
>
> This text is underlined.
>
> ***This text is bold, underlined and in italics.***

Here's how to Make Text Bold

Making text bold is as easy as changing its font. Here's how:

 1 Open the 'Microsoft Word' document 'Dear Father Christmas'.

 2 Select the first sentence — this is what you're going to make bold (see pages 16 and 17).

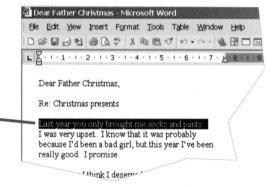

Dear Father Christmas,

Re: Christmas presents

Last year you only brought me socks and pants. I was very upset. I know that it was probably because I'd been a bad girl, but this year I've been really good. I promise.

3 Click on the button at the top of the screen with the B on it.

4 Admire your handiwork. It should look like this.

Re: Christmas presents

Last year you only brought me socks and pants. I was very upset. I know that it was probably because I'd been a bad girl, but this year I've been really good. I promise.

Be bold and try out bold...

Bold is great. It's as easy as just clicking on an icon, and it can make the difference between a dull, drab, boring page and one with bits that stand out. Which is nice.

Bold, Italics and Underline

So now you know how to make text bold. Well, underlining and italicising are just as easy.

Italics are Easy to Create

Here's how to italicise:

 1 <u>Select</u> the last sentence of the first paragraph (see pages 16 and 17).

 2 <u>Click</u> on the button at the top of the screen with the *I* on it.

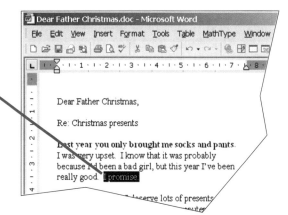

 **3** <u>Check</u> what you've done. It should look like this:

Underlining is Just as Easy

Here's how to underline things:

 1 <u>Select</u> the second line of the document (again, see pages 16 and 17).

 2 <u>Click</u> on the button at the top of the screen with the <u>U</u> on it.

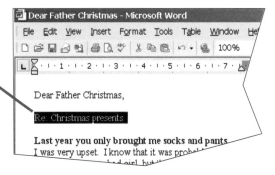

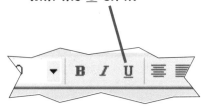 **3** Say '<u>hoorah</u>'. What you've done should look like this:

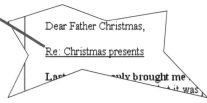

4 <u>Close</u> the file. Click on '<u>No</u>' when it asks if you want to save your changes.

Just for a change, this bit isn't underlined or italicised...

You can also change the colour of your text.
Select the text you want to change, then find this button on the toolbar.
Click on the arrow to choose a different colour.

Font Size

You can change the size of your text, to make it exactly how you want it.

Text Can be Different Sizes

You can make text easier to read if it's larger, or fit more words on a page if it's smaller.
You can use larger text to emphasise important words and phrases too.
Here's how to change font size when you're writing in 'Microsoft Word':

 1 Open 'Microsoft Word' and do a little bit of typing in a new blank document.

 2 You'll see a box which tells you which font size you're
currently using. Click on the arrow next to it.

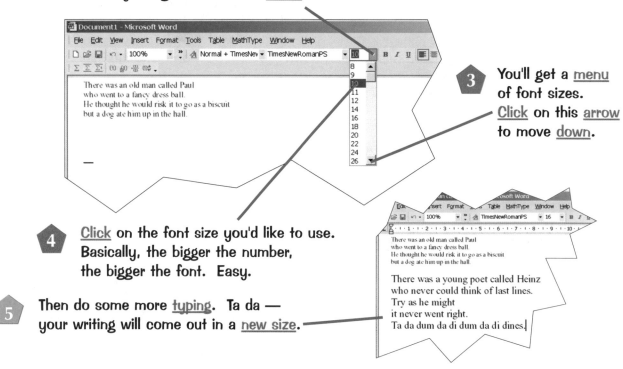

3 You'll get a menu
of font sizes.
Click on this arrow
to move down.

4 Click on the font size you'd like to use.
Basically, the bigger the number,
the bigger the font. Easy.

5 Then do some more typing. Ta da —
your writing will come out in a new size.

You can Change Font Size After You've Typed Things

1 Select the piece of text
you want to change.
(See pages 16 and 17
for how to select text.)

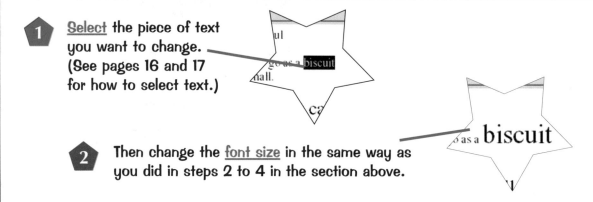

2 Then change the font size in the same way as
you did in steps 2 to 4 in the section above.

Smaller fonts can get hard to read, so be careful...

If you've managed to make things bold, underlined, different fonts etc, you'll have no problems
with changing the font size. It's just about selecting things and clicking on menus. Simple.

Paragraphs

You might have already noticed how you get from one line to the next, but here's how anyway...

When you Type, New Lines Just Appear

On a typewriter, when you got to the end of a line, you'd have to physically move your paper back to the start of the next line. With computers, new lines just happen — it's called 'text wrap'.

 Type some words into a 'Microsoft Word' document.
When you get to the end of a line, you'll see your last word won't fit on...

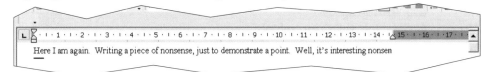

Here I am again. Writing a piece of nonsense, just to demonstrate a point. Well, it's interesting nonsen

 ...but don't panic, just keep typing.
Hey presto, that last word has jumped down automatically onto the next line. Excellent.

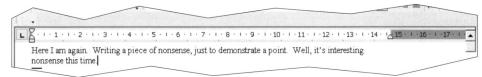

Here I am again. Writing a piece of nonsense, just to demonstrate a point. Well, it's interesting nonsense this time.

Making New Lines and Paragraphs is Easy

 You can start a new line whenever you want just by pressing 'Enter'.

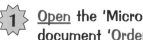

1. Open the 'Microsoft Word' document 'Order Letter'.

The items I would like to order are 5 Aardvark Hammers in neon orange. 7 Centipede Crushers in navy blue. I would be grateful if you could deliver by the 2nd August, as we hope to start the new project as soon as possible. Yours faithfully, Frederick Biggleswade.

 2. Click your mouse here.

 3. Press 'Enter' once to start a new line. (This is called a 'line break'.)

 4. Now click your mouse here.

The items I would like to order are:
5 Aardvark Hammers in neon orange. 7 Centipede Crushers in navy blue. I would be grateful if you could deliver by the 2nd August, as we hope to start the new project as soon as possible. Yours faithfully, Frederick Biggleswade.

 5. Press 'Enter' twice.
You've made a paragraph break (i.e. a line break and 1 linespace).

The items I would like to order are:
5 Aardvark Hammers in neon orange. 7 Centipede Crushers in navy blue.

I would be grateful if you could deliver by the 2nd August, as we hope to start the new project as soon as possible. Yours faithfully, Frederick Biggleswade.

 6. For more practice, try putting another line break in the 2nd line after 'orange', and a paragraph break before 'Yours faithfully'.

Press Enter twice — not exactly rocket science...

If you've had a play in Word, you'll have noticed already that words jump down a line if you keep typing. And making paragraph breaks isn't hard either — just press enter twice.

Alignment and Justification

You might have already heard of alignment and justification — but what do they really mean?

Alignment and Justification are about Lining Up Text

There are only <u>four</u> different ways of arranging your text...

LEFT-ALIGNED

This text is all lined up on the left-hand side.

> <u>Plot for a really good film</u>
>
> <u>Beginning scene</u>: Alarm rings. Sleepy man hits it, yawns, rolls out of bed. Stumbles into the hall, discovering funny green slime under his feet. Stops, looks bemused. Puts his finger in it and sniffs. Thinks. Then pulls gun out of pyjama pocket, puts back against wall and edges towards the bathroom.

RIGHT-ALIGNED

This text is all lined up on the right-hand side.

> <u>Plot for a really good film</u>
>
> <u>Beginning scene</u>: Alarm rings. Sleepy man hits it, yawns, rolls out of bed. Stumbles into the hall, discovering funny green slime under his feet. Stops, looks bemused. Puts his finger in it and sniffs. Thinks. Then pulls gun out of pyjama pocket, puts back against wall and edges towards the bathroom.

CENTRE-ALIGNED

This text is all lined up in the middle.

> <u>Plot for a really good film</u>
>
> <u>Beginning scene</u>: Alarm rings. Sleepy man hits it, yawns, rolls out of bed. Stumbles into the hall, discovering funny green slime under his feet. Stops, looks bemused. Puts his finger in it and sniffs. Thinks. Then pulls gun out of pyjama pocket, puts back against wall and edges towards the bathroom.

JUSTIFIED

Both edges of this text are lined up. Notice how the <u>gaps</u> between words are now a bit <u>random</u> — sometimes big and sometimes small.

> <u>Plot for a really good film</u>
>
> <u>Beginning scene</u>: Alarm rings. Sleepy man hits it, yawns, rolls out of bed. Stumbles into the hall, discovering funny green slime under his feet. Stops, looks bemused. Puts his finger in it and sniffs. Thinks. Then pulls gun out of pyjama pocket, puts back against wall and edges towards the bathroom.

On the next page, you'll find out <u>how to</u> arrange text in these ways.

Dodgy alignment can look very wrong...

You'll find many uses for alignment: Left-alignment is pretty normal and good for most things. Right-alignment is useful for writing your address and the date on letters. Centre-alignment is useful for titles. Justification is good for making things look smart and professional.

Alignment and Justification

Now you know what aligning and justifying are all about, here's how to do them...

Get to Know Your Buttons

There are four buttons you should get to know if you're planning on aligning and justifying. Here they are:

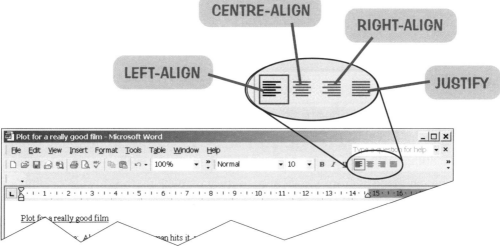

Here's How to Do it

You align and justify just like you make text bold, italic or underlined.

1 Open the Word file '<u>Plot for a really good film</u>'.

2 <u>Select</u> the bit of text that you want to change the <u>alignment</u> of (see pages 16 and 17). This can be just the title, a paragraph, or the whole thing.

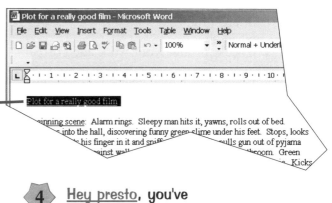

3 <u>Click</u> on the button for whichever <u>aligning</u> or <u>justifying</u> you want to do. (In this case, it's 'centre-align'.)

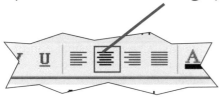

4 <u>Hey presto</u>, you've changed the alignment.

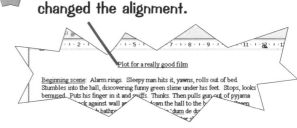

5 <u>Close</u> the file. Click on '<u>No</u>' when it asks if you want to save your changes.

Easy, this alignment lark...

Once you've got the hang of selecting text, you'll be able to change how a piece of text looks, and make it look great. It's easy. You just need to learn which buttons do what.

Section Three — Practice Exercises

The section's not over 'til the practice exercise sings. And here it is, make it sing.

Exercise 1

1. Switch on the computer and monitor correctly and safely.
Wait for the operating system software to load fully.

2. Create a new word processing document.

3. Enter the following text:

Get Active!

Inactivity is causing serious health problems. Physical activity is natural, healthy and improves your physical and mental health. This can mean going swimming, playing a sport or doing everyday things such as walking, climbing the stairs or gardening. Everyone can benefit from physical activity whatever their age, size or physical condition. It is recommended that everyone should do 30 minutes moderate physical activity 5 or more days a week. This may feel too much at first, so start with 5 minutes at least three times a day. Then gradually build up the time and frequency until 30 minutes feels easier.

The British Heart Foundation and The Countryside Agency have joined forces to encourage more people to walk with others from their local community. The "Walking the Way to Health Initiative" (www.whi.org.uk) are helping people to choose, signpost and promote routes for walking. They also help to organise guided walks for those who like to walk in a group. They also provide information on how to make the walks more interesting.

4. Check through your work and correct any obvious errors.

5. Enter your name, centre number and today's date a few lines below the end of the text.

6. Increase the font size of the first sentence in the first paragraph, **Inactivity is causing serious health problems.** so that it is larger than the rest of the text.

7. Save the document with the filename **activity** and print one copy.

8. Insert the following text after the words 'more interesting' in the second paragraph:
   and safe either in the countryside or in an urban area.

9. Insert a paragraph break in the first paragraph after the words 'size or physical condition'.

10. Change only the heading **Get Active!** to a different readable font.

11. Fully justify all the text except the title.

12. Embolden and centre the heading **Get Active!**. Make sure the rest of the text is not bold.

13. Save the document with the new filename **walking** and print one copy.

14. Close the document and exit the application securely.

Section Three — Practice Exercises

...and some more practice. You'll be getting pretty good now...

Exercise 2

1. Open the word processing document called **internet 2.**

2. Increase the font size of the words in the third sentence of the second paragraph, **The World Wide Web**, so it is larger than the rest of the text.

3. Format the heading so that it is larger than the rest of the text.

4. Insert a paragraph break in the second paragraph after the words 'to browse or search for information'.

5. Embolden and centre the heading. Make sure that the rest of the text is not bold.

6. Fully justify all text apart from the heading.

7. Underline and italicise the text **WWW** in the last paragraph, not including the brackets.

8. Save the document with the new filename **internet 3.**

9. Print a final copy of the document.

10. Close the document and exit the application securely.

Exercise 3

1. Open the word processing document called **lakes 2**.

2. Increase the font size of the words **National Park Visitors Centre at Brockhole** in the second paragraph, so that it is larger than the rest of the text.

3. Insert the following text as the last sentence of the second paragraph, after the text 'events throughout the area'.

   There is so much to do and see in the Lake District that you may not want to go home.

4. Insert a paragraph break in the second paragraph after the words 'walking and boating holidays'.

5. Change only the heading to a different readable font and increase the font size.

6. Fully justify all the text.

7. Embolden and centre the heading. Make sure the rest of the text is not bold.

8. Save the document with the new filename **lakes 3** and print one copy.

9. Close the document and exit the application securely.

Moving Text

Word-processors let you move text around on the page. Here's one way to do this...

You can *Move Text* by *Clicking* and *Dragging*

 1 Open the 'Microsoft Word' document 'Slug Collectors Monthly'.

 2 Select the first paragraph of
'Slug Collectors Monthly'
(see pages 16 and 17 if you're not sure how).

Slug Collectors Monthly

The next meeting of the Slug Collectors' Society will be held on the 14th June.
All members with a new species to report should fill in the relevant paperwork beforehand.
If you are bringing slugs with you, please ensure that you wipe the slime off the chairs afterwards.

Annual Outing

This year's outing was to a field near Slough. The coach set off early, and there was a lot of excitement in the air as we approached our destination. The dew was still on the grass when we arrived, which led to a record number of sightings. We were delighted to see that *Sybil* the big black slug was still in residence, and we made the acquaintance of many of her charming offspring. We look forward to seeing many more of them next year.

Reminder: any member caught with slug pellets or salt in their possession will be banned from the Society. Feeding slugs to ducks, or stamping on them will also be treated as a disciplinary offence.

 3 Move your mouse over the highlighted text
until the cursor changes to an arrow.

 4 Click the left mouse button and hold it down.

Keep holding down the left mouse button —
the exercise continues on the next page.

Ray spent years training
his pet slug to lie quietly
on his upper lip.

Moving Text

 5 Keep the mouse button <u>held down</u>, and <u>drag</u> it to the gap between the second and third paragraphs.

Slug Collectors Monthly

The next meeting of the Slug Collectors' Society will be held on the 14th June. All members with a new species to report should fill in the relevant paperwork beforehand. If you are bringing slugs with you, please ensure that you wipe the slime off the chairs afterwards.

Annual Outing

This year's outing was to a field near Slough. The coach set off early, and there was a lot of excitement in the air as we approached our destination. The dew was still on the grass when we arrived, which led to a record number of sightings. We were delighted to see that *Sybil* the big black slug was still in residence, and we made the acquaintance of many of her charming offspring. We look forward to seeing many more of them next year.

Reminder: any member caught with slug pellets or salt in their possession will be banned from the Society. Feeding slugs to ducks, or stamping on them will also be treated as a disciplinary offence.

6 When the <u>arrow</u> is pointing to where you want the text to be, <u>let go</u> of the mouse button.

Slug Collectors Monthly

Annual Outing

This year's outing was to a field near Slough. The coach set off early, and there was a lot of excitement in the air as we approached our destination. The dew was still on the grass when we arrived, which led to a record number of sightings. We were delighted to see that *Sybil* the big black slug was still in residence, and we made the acquaintance of many of her charming offspring. We look forward to seeing many more of them next year.

The next meeting of the Slug Collectors' Society will be held on the 14th June. All members with a new species to report should fill in the relevant paperwork beforehand. If you are bringing slugs with you, please ensure that you wipe the slime off the chairs afterwards.

Reminder: any member caught with slug pellets or salt in their possession will be banned from the Society. Feeding slugs to ducks, or stamping on them will also be treated as a disciplinary offence.

The highlighted text has moved.

 7 <u>Close</u> the document but <u>don't</u> save the changes you made.

Don't worry if you make a mistake — you can "undo" it...

If you make a mistake, you can "undo" your last change. Go to the 'Edit' menu at the top of the screen and click on 'Undo Move'. This will take the text back to how it was before your last change. Undo is a really handy trick and will work in most situations, not just with moving text.

Moving Text

There are lots of different ways to move text around on the page.
Now you've got the hang of clicking and dragging, have a go at cutting, copying and pasting.

You can Cut and Paste Text

 1 Open the 'Microsoft Word' document 'Dear Mr Higgins'.

 2 Select the third paragraph (see pages 16 and 17).

 3 Click on the 'Edit' menu, then click on 'Cut'. This removes the highlighted text, just like cutting it out with scissors.

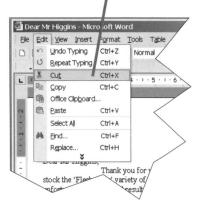

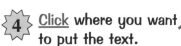 **4** Click where you want to put the text.

 5 Click on the 'Edit' menu on the toolbar, then click on 'Paste'. This pops the text into its new location.

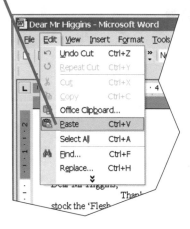

 6 Close the document. (Don't save the changes you made.)

There's no need for scissors or glue...

When you cut something out, it doesn't really disappear — the computer just stores it on something called the clipboard until you paste it somewhere else. Clever.

Copying Text

That's all very well, but what if you just want to make a copy of part of your text? Read on...

You can also Copy and Paste Text

 Open the 'Microsoft Word' document 'Things to do this week'.

 Select the words 'Buy baked beans.'

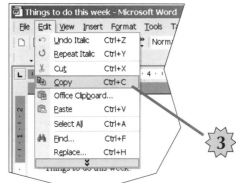

Things to do this week:

Monday: Wash socks.
Tuesday: Buy baked beans.
Wednesday: Write a letter of complaint to the Prime Minister.
Thursday: Go to a tortoise fight.
Friday: Read *War and Peace*.
Saturday: Wash socks.
Sunday:

3 Click on the 'Edit' menu on the toolbar, and click on 'Copy'. This leaves the text where it is, but makes a copy of it.

4 Click where you want to put the text.

Things to do this week:

Monday: Wash socks.
Tuesday: Buy baked beans.
Wednesday: Write a letter of complaint to the Prime Minister.
Thursday: Go to a tortoise fight.
Friday: Read *War and Peace*.
Saturday: Wash socks.
Sunday:|

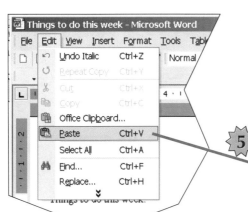

5 Click on the 'Edit' menu on the toolbar, then click on 'Paste'.

A copy of the words will be pasted in the new location.

Always wanted to have twins?
— just copy and paste.

Things to do this week:

Monday: Wash socks.
Tuesday: Buy baked beans.
Wednesday: Write a letter of complaint to the Prime Minister.
Thursday: Go to a tortoise fight.
Friday: Read *War and Peace*.
Saturday: Wash socks.
Sunday: Buy baked beans.|

 Close the document without saving your changes.

Don't get in a sticky mess...

Cutting, copying and pasting are really handy skills — but not as useful as knowing how to swim, or change a plug, or ride a bike, or milk a badger... actually, forget that last one.

Find and Replace

Find and Replace is a really handy tool that lets you make lots of
changes to a document at once. Perfect if you're always in a hurry.

'Replace' Lets you Swap One Word for Another

Say you want to change the word 'slug' to 'snail' in your document (snails are nicer):

1 Open the 'Microsoft Word' document '<u>Slug Collectors Monthly</u>'.

2 Click on the '<u>Edit</u>' menu, then click on '<u>Replace</u>'.

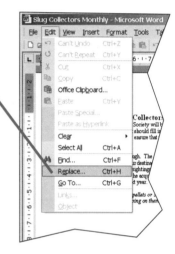

3 You'll see a menu like the one below.
Type the word you want to find here, '<u>slug</u>'.

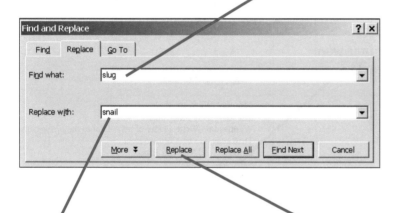

4 Type the new word
'<u>snail</u>', here.

5 Now click '<u>Replace</u>'. The computer
will find the word 'slug' in your text,
and highlight it.

6 Click '<u>Replace</u>' again to change it to '<u>snail</u>'
and move on to the <u>next word</u>.

7 When you get to this word, you don't
want to change it, because the product
is called '<u>slug pellets</u>'. Click on '<u>Find
Next</u>' to skip it and go to the <u>next word</u>.

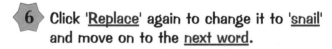

caught with **slug** *pellets or salt*
to ducks, or stamping on them w

8 <u>Close</u> the document (don't save your changes).

Your computer can't think for itself...yet...

You can click 'Replace All' to replace all the words at once, but it's usually best to
just use 'Replace' so the computer doesn't change words you don't want to change.

Spell Checking

Word-processors can help you spell things correctly and use proper grammar.

Spellcheckers Find Mistakes

'Microsoft Word' usually <u>underlines</u> your <u>spelling</u> and <u>grammar</u> mistakes for you.

1 Open the Word document '<u>Spelling Practice</u>'.

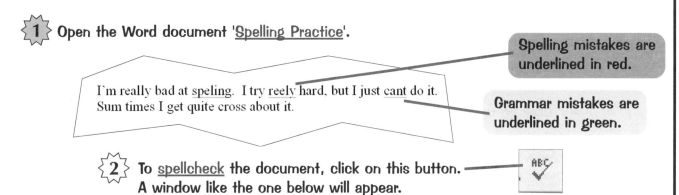

I'm really bad at speling. I try reely hard, but I just cant do it.
Sum times I get quite cross about it.

Spelling mistakes are underlined in red.

Grammar mistakes are underlined in green.

2 To <u>spellcheck</u> the document, click on this button.
A window like the one below will appear.

This shows the misspelled word.

This is a list of suggestions to replace the misspelled word.

3 Click on the word you want to <u>replace</u> it with.

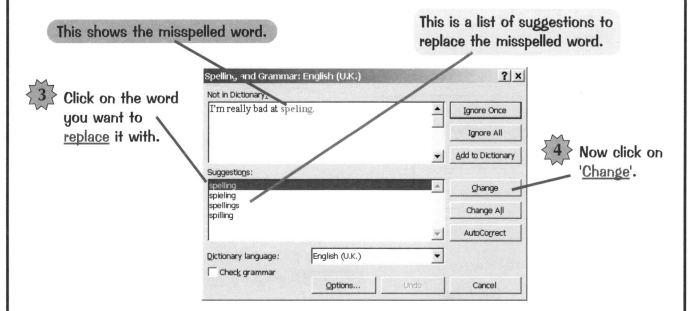

Spelling and Grammar: English (U.K.)

Not in Dictionary:
I'm really bad at speling.

Ignore Once
Ignore All
Add to Dictionary

Suggestions:
spelling
spieling
spellings
spilling

Change
Change All
AutoCorrect

Dictionary language: English (U.K.)
☐ Check grammar

Options... | Undo | Cancel

4 Now click on '<u>Change</u>'.

If you look at the document now, '<u>speling</u>' will have become '<u>spelling</u>'.

Spellcheckers Can't Find All Mistakes

You have to be careful with spellcheckers — they can't find <u>every</u> mistake — this should say '<u>sometimes</u>', but because '<u>sum</u>' and '<u>times</u>' are both <u>real words</u>, the spellchecker thinks they're <u>OK</u>.

I'm really bad at speling. I try reely hard, but I just cant do it.
Sum times I get quite cross about it.

Thare's sumfing rong wif mi spelchekur...

Spellcheckers are handy, but they're not going to spot everything.
Always print your work and check it yourself to make sure it makes sense.

Margins

Margins are the parts of the page round the edges of the text.
As part of the assessment you need to know how to change the left and right margins.

You can Change the Page Margins

1 Open the document '<u>Dear Miss Choggleswink</u>'.

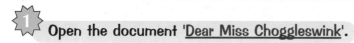

2 Click on the '<u>File</u>' menu, then click on '<u>Page Setup</u>'.

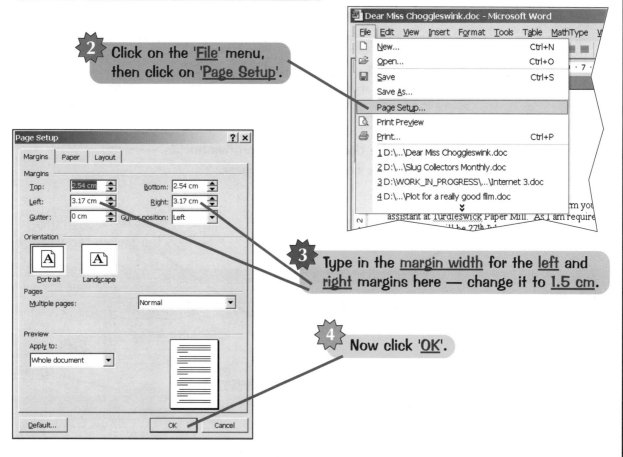

3 Type in the <u>margin width</u> for the <u>left</u> and <u>right</u> margins here — change it to <u>1.5 cm</u>.

4 Now click '<u>OK</u>'.

5 Now try it again — <u>this time</u>, change the left and right margin width to <u>4 cm</u>.

1.5 cm left margin

4 cm left margin

This will come in handy for the assessment...

Usually you just use a document with the margins already set up, but you need to know how to change them for the assessment. So what are you waiting for? Get margining I tell you.

Line Spacing

It can be hard to read text when it's all crammed together... so it's better to space it out a bit.

You can Change the Spacing between the Lines

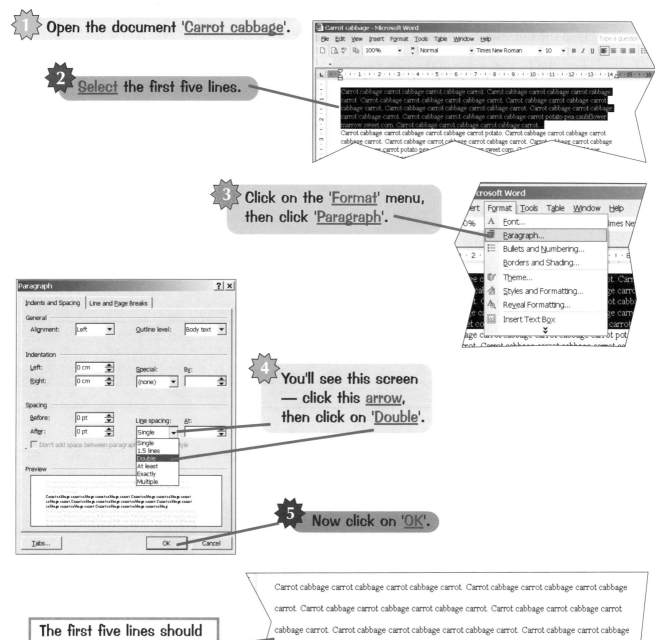

1 Open the document 'Carrot cabbage'.

2 Select the first five lines.

3 Click on the 'Format' menu, then click 'Paragraph'.

4 You'll see this screen — click this arrow, then click on 'Double'.

5 Now click on 'OK'.

The first five lines should now be double-spaced.

Mind the gap...

Before we end this section, here's a quick reminder of a really useful editing tool — "undo". Everything you do in this section can be undone, so if you make a mistake with any of it, remember — go to the 'Edit' menu and select the 'Undo...' option. It really is a life-saver...

Section Four — Practice Exercises

There are a lot of things to practise in this section.
Work your way through these exercises until you're confident with them all.

Exercise 1

1. Open the document with the filename **walking**.

2. Move the last sentence of the first paragraph,

   > Everyone can benefit from physical activity whatever their age, size or physical condition.

   to become the last sentence of the second paragraph.

3. Replace all occurrences of the word **activity** with the word **exercise** (three times in all).

4. Change the left and right margins to 5 cm.

5. Set the last paragraph only in double line spacing.

6. Save the document with the new filename **getactive** and print one copy.

7. Close the document and exit the application securely.

Exercise 2

1. Open the document with the filename called **internet 3**.

2. Move the last sentence of the first paragraph,

   > When you are connected to the Internet you can then communicate with other computers and exchange information.

   to become the first sentence of the last paragraph.

3. Replace all occurrences of the word **connected** with the word **linked** (three times in all).

4. Change the left and right margins to 4 cm.

5. Set the first paragraph only in double line spacing.

6. Save the document with the new filename **internet 4** and print one copy.

7. Close the document and exit the application securely.

Section Four — Practice Exercises

Here are a couple more exercises to keep you entertained.
All this practice should help you fly through your assessment.

Exercise 3

1.   Open the word processing document called **maths2**.

2.   Move the first paragraph so that it becomes the last paragraph.

3.   Replace all occurrences of the word **lesson** with the word **class** (three times in all).

4.   Change the left and right margins to 3.5cm.

5.   Set ALL the paragraphs in double line spacing.

6.   Enter your name, centre number and today's date a few lines below the end of the text.

7.   Save the document with the new filename **maths3** and print one copy.

8.   Close the document and exit the application securely.

Exercise 4

1.   Open your word processing document called **lakes 3**.

2.   Move the last sentence of the first paragraph,

> There are impressive mountains, rolling fells, relaxing lakes and busy market towns.

to become the fourth sentence of the first paragraph.

3.   Replace all occurrences of the word **miles** with the word **kilometres** (two times in all).

4.   Change the left and right margins to 5cm.

5.   Set the first paragraph only in double line spacing.

6.   Save the document with the new filename **lakes 4** and print one copy.

7.   Close the document and exit the application securely.

Advice for the Assessment

Once you've <u>completed</u> the course, you should be ready to take the <u>assessment</u>.
Here are a couple of pages of handy <u>advice</u> to help you out.
You've probably heard it before, but read it again — it's useful stuff.

You'll get 2 Hours to Complete the Assessment

You've got <u>plenty</u> of time to do the assessment, so...

- Don't <u>panic</u>.

  - Don't <u>rush</u> — you'll make mistakes.

    - Read the <u>instructions</u> properly, and make sure you <u>follow</u> them.

      - <u>Check</u> your work as you go along, especially your <u>typing</u>.

        - <u>Don't</u> panic. (Did I already mention that?)

Avoid these Errors

If you make a <u>major error</u>, like failing to do one of the <u>tasks</u> in the assessment, you <u>won't pass</u>.
So, make sure you follow the instructions <u>carefully</u>.

If you make <u>more than three</u> minor errors, you won't pass the assessment either.
So, <u>avoid</u> making small mistakes like these:

1) Making a <u>typing</u> (<u>data entry</u>) error in the data you're asked to enter.

2) Failing to use <u>capital letters</u> appropriately.

3) Using more than one <u>linespace</u> between paragraphs, or pressing <u>Enter</u> unnecessarily.

4) Saving with the wrong <u>filename</u>.

5) Not typing your <u>name</u>, <u>centre number</u> and the <u>date</u> on your documents.
   (You <u>won't</u> lose marks if you make <u>typing errors</u> in this information.)

Watch Out for Data Entry Errors

When you're asked to type something, <u>make sure</u> you type it <u>exactly</u> as it's written,
with the right <u>spacing</u> and <u>punctuation</u> — otherwise you're just throwing easy marks away.

<u>Print</u> your documents to check for errors, then <u>correct</u>
them on the computer before you hand them in.

Just relax and you'll be fine...

If you've prepared for the assessment properly, you won't have anything to worry about.
You just have to show what you can do, without making any silly mistakes.

Advice for the Assessment

Check that you Know How to Do these Things

All you need to know to pass the assessment is in this book.
Use the checklist below to make sure you're confident with all the tasks you could
be asked to do. Go back and look at the relevant pages again if you're not sure.

1)	Open, close, save and print Word documents.	Pages 12-13
2)	Change the left and right margins.	Page 34
3)	Enter text, numbers and symbols accurately.	Page 10
4)	Select text.	Pages 16-17
5)	Delete text.	Page 11
6)	Change the font of selected text.	Page 19
7)	Embolden, underline and italicise selected text.	Pages 20-21
8)	Change the size of selected text.	Page 22
9)	Align text to the left, right or centre, or justify text.	Page 25
10)	Insert paragraph breaks.	Page 23
11)	Cut, copy and paste selected text.	Pages 30-31
12)	Select and move text using the mouse.	Pages 28-29
13)	Make alterations using 'Find and Replace'.	Page 32
14)	Alter the line spacing.	Page 35
15)	Check your spelling using the spellchecker.	Page 33

You're so close to the end... Just one little test to do...

Once you've ticked all the boxes, you're ready for some practice assessments.
There's one over the page to get you started.

Section Five — Practice Assessment

Here's a practice assessment for you to try. This will be pretty similar to the test you'll get when you've finished your course. So if you can do this, you shouldn't have any problems with the real thing. Have a go — see how you do.

Scenario

You are working as an editorial assistant in a wildlife organisation. Your job is to create and format articles for inclusion in a monthly newsletter and for local newspapers.

Your editor has asked you to produce a document about wasps.

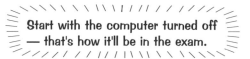

Start with the computer turned off — that's how it'll be in the exam.

1. Switch on the computer and monitor correctly and safely.
    Wait for the operating system software to load fully.

2. Create a new word processing document.

3. Set the left and right margins to 2.5 cm.

4. Enter the following text, making sure that it is left-aligned only:

> Wasps - More Good than Harm
>
> Of all the insects found in the British garden, the common wasp, Vespula Vulgaris, is probably one of the most hated. Not many of us can have gone through a season without being annoyed by wasps buzzing around our ice cream. Most of us at some time or another will also have felt the sharp pain of a sting.
>
> Wasps are only responding to their instincts, and our excessive use of sugar. Normally, wasps are carnivorous throughout the season. They will feed on other insects. It is not uncommon to see a wasp with a caterpillar in its mouth. It is only at the end of the season, when their preferred food source begins to run low, that they turn to any rotting fruit that lies around on the floor. So when you are enjoying your BBQ and you are getting pestered, remember, the wasps are only after a good source of sugar.
>
> A wasp will scour plants for other insect pests, and when their prey is paralysed they will take them away. When you consider that a wasp nest may have as many as 10,000 workers by the end of September, each of which will have been fed on its own insect pest, you begin to see how much work the wasps do in the garden.

Section Five — Practice Assessment

Here's the rest... Carry on — you can do it.

5. Enter your name, centre number and today's date a few lines below the end of the text.

6. Format the heading so that it is larger than the rest of the text.

7. Save your document with the filename **wasps** and print one copy.

The editor has asked for amendments to be made to the document.

8. Insert a paragraph break and clear linespace in the second paragraph after the words ....**in its mouth**.

9. Insert the following text as the second sentence of the third paragraph, after the words ...**around on the floor**.

The wasps then become drunk on the fermenting fruit.

10. Move the first sentence of the last paragraph, **A wasp will scour plants for other insect pests, and when their prey is paralysed they will take them away.** to become the fourth sentence of the second paragraph.

11. Delete the last sentence of the second paragraph, **It is not uncommon to see a wasp with a caterpillar in its mouth.**

12. Replace all occurrences of the word **season** with the word **summer** (three times in all).

13. Make the words Vespula Vulgaris italic.

14. Change only the heading **Wasps - More Good than Harm** to a different readable font.

15. Fully justify all the text below the heading.

16. Embolden and centre the heading **Wasps - More Good than Harm**.
Make sure that the rest of the text is not bold.

17. Change the left and right margins to 4 cm.

18. Set the first paragraph only in double linespacing.

19. Save the document with the new filename **vespula** and print one copy.

20. Close the document and exit the application securely.

Index